Parenting Your Anxious Child

Practical Ways to Help Your Anxious Child Overcome Worry, Shyness and Social Anxiety

Larissa Harvey

©Copyright 2022 – Larissa Harvey - All rights reserved

The content contained within this book may not be reproduced, duplicated, or transmitted without direct written permission from the author or the publisher.

Under no circumstances will any blame or legal responsibility be held against the publisher, or author, for any damages, reparation, or monetary loss due to the information contained within this book, either directly or indirectly.

Legal Notice

This book is copyright protected. This book is only for personal use. You cannot amend, distribute, sell, use, quote or paraphrase any part, or the content within this book, without the consent of the author-publisher.

Disclaimer Notice

Please note the information contained within this document is for educational and entertainment purposes only. All effort has been executed to present accurate, up to date, and reliable, complete information. No warranties of any kind are declared or implied. Readers acknowledge that the author is not engaging in the rendering of legal, financial, medical, or professional advice.

Table of Contents

Introduction 4

How to Get the Most Out of this book 7

Chapter 1: Anxiety – What It Is and How It Often Presents Itself in Children 10

Chapter 2: The Reality of Raising an Anxious Child 21

Chapter 3: What Are The Causes of Anxiety in Children? 31

Chapter 4: What Could Possibly Happen To Your Child If You Don't Do Anything? 42

Chapter 5: What You Can Do To Help Your Child Overcome His Anxiety 53

Chapter 6: What You Can Say to Help Your Child Become Less Anxious 64

Chapter 7: Dos and Don'ts of Raising an Anxious Child (With Examples and FAQs) 74

Chapter 8: How You Should React In the Face of Progress (Or Setbacks) 86

Chapter 9: The Importance of Patience and Positivity 95

Chapter 10: What You Must Do When Your Child Finally Stops Being Anxious 105

Conclusion 113

Introduction

Parenting is one of the hardest things that you will ever do. But it can also be one of the best, most wonderful, and most rewarding experiences of your life.

Now, when you have a child with anxiety, parenting can be particularly challenging. That is because you have to do things a bit differently than you normally would, at least until your child overcomes this phase of their life, which brings us to the motive behind the writing of this book.

Childhood anxiety doesn't have to define the rest of your beloved child's life, does it?

There is absolutely no reason why your child's social anxiety or separation fears should follow them all the way into adulthood. There is no law or rule that states that must absolutely be the case.

People do overcome things, and in my own limited capacity as a fellow parent, I have learned that children are the most resilient souls that this world has to offer. If anyone can overcome the grueling, gnawing monster that is anxiety, children can. And in following that rule of thumb, your anxious child most definitely can.

In this world of ups and downs, and – ugh! –social media and the internet, the responsibility of bringing up a child falls largely to the parent. It is left to us to ensure that our little angels grow up to become well-adjusted adults, responsible adults who are capable of living their very best lives without hang-ups and insecurities nipping at their heels at every turn. And so, we must not neglect our responsibilities.

What you will find in this book, *Raising an Anxious Child*, includes:

- The true meaning of anxiety in children, from your child's perspective, and its effects on reality (yours and theirs)
- The causes of anxiety in children, and how you can determine them in your unique child
- The possible psychological effects of anxiety in your child's life, in the long term.
- What you can do to help your child. Basically, we will be looking at time-tested and psychologically proven strategies mostly in this book. These include action plans and words – strong words of encouragement – that your child needs to hear to improve their confidence.
- What you should do in the aftermath. Anxiety can be hard to overcome, and it likes to slink its way back in if you don't continue to be on your guard. You must help your child do this and remain free from anxiety once success is achieved. And so, this book will help you.

Finally, it is never easy to help someone with anxiety, especially a child. It can be frustrating, but you must stay motivated and encouraged along the way; so as not to sabotage your own mental health along the way. The only way to guarantee this, however, is to remain positive. Be gentle with your child, go easy on yourself, don't give up, and you will surely see the results.

How to Get the Most Out of this book

There are 3 important things that you must do – and keep in mind – if you are to get your money's worth from this book. They are:

- **Read:** Of course, you must read this book. How else will you know what I'm talking about? And by "read," I do not mean you should aimlessly flip through the pages like you might do with a magazine. No. You. Must. Read. This. Book.
  Find a good time, get comfortable and...read.
- **Meditate**: This is a tricky one. My suggestion is for you to do your reading with a small notebook and a pen. Jot down important points that will be made on social anxiety and relate them to your child's behavior. You may begin with something like, "Separation anxiety – Georgie doesn't want to go to school..."
  Basically, you must try to *really* identify your child's displays of anxiety. And then, you must try to figure out the underlying causes behind them. If possible, come up with a plan on how to discuss them gently with your child.
- **Apply:** There are several lessons, instructions, and even strategies to be learned from this book on how to raise your anxious child. You must apply them.
  You must know that there is no universal, one-shoe-fits-all rule to raising children, even those who have anxiety in common.

So, it is left to you, the parent, to figure out how best to apply these crucial lessons uniquely to your child, to help them overcome their childhood anxiety.

Again, I will tell you: It won't be easy. But it will be worth it. You'll see.

Chapter 1:
Anxiety – What It Is and How It Often Presents Itself in Children

What is anxiety?

This is perhaps the most essential question in this book. The next most important question would be, "Does your child have anxiety?" But we'll get to that in a little while. First, we must describe anxiety.

The disorder – or condition, if you will – is easy enough to define. According to the NHS (The National Health Service), it is "a feeling of unease, such as worry or fear, that can be mild or severe."

The British Psychological Society terms it "a feeling of profound agitation and unease about an imminent unpleasant experience, often accompanied by physical symptoms such as breathlessness, sweating, and a racing heartbeat." They also say that "in the most severe cases, these symptoms can be extremely debilitating."

One more definition I would like to add before we go on is the one given by the American Psychological Society. While they describe anxiety as "a normal reaction to stress," they also state that anxiety disorders are very different from the usual nerves that are common to most people. In fact, what they say precisely is, "Anxiety disorders differ from normal feelings of nervousness or anxiousness, and involve excessive fear or anxiety." They also say that anxiety disorders are "the most common of mental disorders and affect nearly 30 percent of adults at some point in their lives."

Now, what all this simply means is that anxiety is a big deal. It is serious. It is a real medical condition, a disorder. You can't sweep it under the rug or wish it away, or ignore it in hopes that it will magically disappear like Cinderella's beautiful carriage at twelve midnight.

The "let's-do-nothing-but-hope-they-outgrow-it" approach will probably, most definitely not work here. Anxiety is real. And this is the first thing that you must know about it.

The second thing that you absolutely have to know is that anxiety wears many faces and can manifest in different ways, in both adults and children.

If you're looking to find answers in this book for an adult (or an adult child), you will probably end up with some pointers or helpful tips because anxiety somehow manages to bring out the child in us. However, this book is geared specifically towards children and was written with them in mind.

Anxiety in children – or child anxiety – can occur in many different ways. The most probable reason for this is that most children have a very strong sense of imagination. They are also renowned for their innocence. So, with their particular demographic – or at least with children from ages 0-12 – you're likely to get a great deal of honesty in your dealings with them. They don't usually have emotional walls up, and those that do have probably not learned to fortify them well. So, what you have with children is usually the raw form of human nature, without walls, rock-steady pretense, and guile. More than 80% of the time, what you see is what you get.

In most instances, your children will show you their true feelings, with an awe-inspiring lack of guardedness that will humble you. Because of this, as a parent, you get to experience all those feelings right along with them – from the joys of taking their very first step and the sense of achievement that comes with getting their very first A on their school exams to the terror of their very first nightmare and the absolute helplessness of those first stirrings of anxiety.

Being a parent is not always easy. I've said it before and will say it again: Being a parent is one of the hardest things you will ever do. The sense of responsibility that comes with it is crushing, even more so than the job itself at times, and we must constantly deal with the need to fix everything in our children's lives to make an imperfect world perfect for them. So, their achievements become our achievements, and their fears become our fears. And their anxiety...well, let's just say there is a reason why you're currently reading this book.

When anxiety first rears its ugly head in an anxious child's life, as parents, we do all that we can for them to make it go away. Initially, we may try the good old "let's-do-nothing-but-hope-they-outgrow-it"
approach, our reasoning being that our children are children after all. They are young - the most resilient stock that humanity has to offer - and they will beat this.

While doing this, we may think back to our own childhood fears and terrors. We may remember how we ourselves used to be afraid of the dark and the disdain we used to have for closing our eyes at night...we may even think about how we used to wet our beds when we were that age. And then, we will tell ourselves that it's all normal. After all, we too used to hate being alone at some point...even though we can't really remember when. We continue to rationalize and normalize, and we're quite good at it.

But what happens if that good old do-nothing approach doesn't work? How do you help your child then?

The first way to help your child – the very first thing that you must do to arm yourself and to prepare – is to gather knowledge. Gather as much knowledge about anxiety disorders in children as you possibly can. I assume that that is why you're reading this book, and I applaud you for it.

So, let us get right to it.

As stated earlier, anxiety in children can occur in many different ways. And having established cogent reasons why, along with your own possible reasons for caring – because it is always wise to know exactly why you're doing things, even as a parent – we will proceed.

The common signs of anxiety in children are incessant crying, clinginess, frequently being upset, obvious and constant refusal to talk or play with other children, frequent absences from school, and the big one, fear. This fear is usually undeniable. It can be seen in the anxious child's shaky fingers and clammy hands, increased heart-rate, red face, and shortness of breath, particularly when confronted with the source – or sources – of their anxiety.

Now, all these symptoms can be divided into 6 major classifications of child anxiety disorders, all of which are entirely treatable. They are:

- **Separation anxiety disorder**

SAD is a form of anxiety that happens naturally in babies and very young children. It involves the exhibition of a lot of restlessness when their parents are not around for short durations of time, and perhaps a little fear.

These emotions are usually pronounced when the child is dropped off at daycare or at school, with teachers, peers, or caregivers they are unfamiliar with. Quite simply put, they will look for you when you are not around because they do not wish to be apart from you, and they will cry and throw tantrums for the sake of passing across that message to anybody around. And that is why many children cry on their first day at daycare or at school.

However, if you're lucky, you may notice that things are not so bad on the second day of school or the day after. A week later, you might even find it hard to believe that this was the same child that was clinging to you so tightly on that very first day.

But what if things don't get better and the anxious child doesn't stop throwing tantrums whenever they are to be apart from you? What if their restlessness and fear actually worsen as time progresses? What if they also come up with various scenarios that have them blindingly convinced that "something bad" will happen – either to themselves or their parents – upon separation, even if it's only for a short time?
Well then, that child is said to have separation anxiety disorder or SAD.

- **Specific phobia**

This type of anxiety is one of the easiest to detect in terms of its cause (or causes). When an anxious child has a specific phobia, they are usually terrified or overly anxious about just one thing (or a few specific things); this could be storms, heavy mists, loud noises, clowns, spiders or bugs, blood, needles, doctors, the dark, monsters, shadows, heights, dogs, cats, bread, their own reflections...the list is endless. They will freeze up, cry or throw tantrums when they see these things or are forced to interact with them. They will also go to great lengths to avoid situations where they have to come into contact with the cause – or causes – of their extreme anxiety or phobia.

Though relatively easy to diagnose, specific phobia isn't easier to deal with than other forms of child anxiety because you never know just where or when the object of your child's anxiety will turn up. And then, how will you help them deal with it? What if you're not even there to help them?

Well, as stated earlier, gathering knowledge is the first step to helping your anxious kid, and if you've managed to get this far, then you're on the right path.

- **Selective mutism**

This is an anxiety disorder that is common in children around the age of 5. SM usually presents itself in the anxious child's unwillingness to speak when they are forced into certain social or emotional situations that they feel uncomfortable in. Sometimes, they may not be forced into those situations, but the absence of coercion does not, in fact, make them more at ease.

Such situations include school, a new place of residence (in which case the child may be unwilling to speak to unfamiliar children of new neighbors), a new country, and any other uncomfortable situation you can think of.

Quite simply put, the anxious child is simply too anxious to talk. Can you imagine that kind of fear, the kind that chokes up a child and steals all their words? Well, that is the anxious child's reality when they suffer from selective mutism.

The only bright side – if we can call it that – is that the child will usually revert back to their usual (cheerful) selves whenever they are removed from the uncomfortable situation and are back home with their family and close friends, inside their comfort zone.

Former Miss England, Kirsty Heslewood, stated that she used to suffer from this anxiety disorder as a child, and just look, she turned out fine.

- **Social anxiety disorder (or social phobia)**

This type of anxiety presents itself as fear – or rather, the extreme fear – of being the focus of attention. You might not notice it quickly if you have a large family and your anxious child is very comfortable at home. You may only see that they tend to be very reserved in general or around guests.

However, social anxiety tends to unfurl its dreadful wings in the anxious child's life in school. They will not be able to interact well with their classmates because of the extreme fear of rejection.

To the anxious child, group activities will morph into a brand new form of torture. School presentations – particularly the ones that involve them standing before the entire class or school – will become something to dread. And so, these children will isolate themselves from their peers. They will not just hesitate but hold back from answering questions in class. Sometimes, they will even freeze up or cry when they are called upon to answer questions or are forced into situations they find incredibly uncomfortable.

- **Panic disorder**

This is an extreme form of anxiety that involves sudden occurrences – and reoccurrences – of panic attack episodes. These episodes are characterized by fear, and a dreadful, horrible feeling that "something bad" is about to happen, shortness of breath, increased heart rate, nausea, dizziness, shaky and clammy hands, headaches, chest pains, and a whole host of other symptoms that can last for several minutes at a time. The most pressing concern during this time for the child is the ability to breathe. Because, sometimes – usually – what a panic attack does is convincing you (rather, your anxious child) that you can't breathe. And that is a terrible thing, a terrible feeling because once the mind believes it, the body will usually react accordingly. That is why so many anxious children will pass out when they suffer extreme episodes of panic attacks.

Rest easy, dear parent; it is treatable. Your child can overcome this. After all, as I've said over and over, children are the most resilient stock that humanity has to offer.

- **Generalized anxiety disorder**

GAD is the final classification of child anxiety that we will be examining in this chapter, and it is also one of the most challenging.

When your child suffers from GAD, it is one of the most heartbreaking things to watch. Because, rather than simply being a child and enjoying childhood, they worry about everything.

They worry about their grades, worry about their friendships, worry about the rain, worry about you, worry about how you're doing at your job, worry about the sunrise and the sunset....and often, worry from sunrise to sunset.

This means that they are constantly worrying, and because of that, they are always tired, restless, and irritable. They get headaches from their unfathomable worries and have trouble sleeping at night. And it is not just one thing draining them; it is everything.

As adults, we know very well that life is imperfect, but we are also aware that it is a continuous thing – a continuous effort – to focus on the good parts and the things that actually matter. A child suffering from generalized anxiety disorder does not know that, so they become Atlas of ancient Greek mythology, bent at the knees, with the weight of the world resting squarely on their small shoulders.

If you've read through this chapter and you've also meditated and taken notes, you will find that your anxious child's symptoms fall into one – or more– of the above 6 classifications.

However, if you feel that your child's symptoms do not fit into any of the above disorders highlighted above, you must still gather knowledge.

Soldier on, dear parent.

Chapter 2:
The Reality of Raising an Anxious Child

It is not an easy thing to raise a child who is suffering from anxiety. And that is because the worst truth about anxiety – the sad reality of this disorder- is that it is debilitating. Quite simply put, anxiety can eat deep into the life of a child. Once it does this, it will usually slow the child down, making things that should come naturally extremely difficult, in many cases.

This disorder gets inside the anxious child's head and plants the seeds of doubt whenever they happen to come in contact with the object of their anxiety or whenever they are put in uncomfortable situations.

As stated in the previous chapter, many of us suffer from nerves whenever we are placed in uncomfortable situations; that twinge of unease on the first day of school (or work, in our case), that feeling of nervousness in our belly whenever we have to give a speech in front of a crowd, that unease whenever we feel like we're wearing too much make-up or the wrong clothes in an important place, and so many other instances of uncomfortable situations. However, our sense of unease does not usually make us freeze up, nor does it render us incapable of carrying out what we need to do in those situations. That is because our discomfort isn't debilitating. But that is not the case for your child.

If your child is suffering from separation anxiety disorder (SAD), they will not want to be away from you or their other caregivers for too long. They will be unable to do so due to the sort of anxiety they suffer from, and so, they will cry and throw tantrums whenever any form of separation looms on the horizon. They will crawl into bed with you, with or without your permission, and no matter how well you try to hide, they will always – always – find you.

It can be very difficult to deal with this kind of almost stalker-ish behavior from your own child. You can't even describe it as "cute" because of the overwhelming terror that you see in their eyes whenever you even suggest that you have to leave them alone for any considerable length of time, even when it's just for school.

But what is really running through your child's mind in those moments? What are they so afraid of?

Depending on how forthcoming your child is about their SAD, you might get answers like:

- Something bad will happen if you leave me.
- Mommy, Daddy, I don't want you to go.
- What if aliens come and take you away?
- What if you leave me and never come back.

All these thoughts are circling in the anxious child's head, and sometimes, they might know in their heads – logically – that their fear is unreasonable. But reason rarely has an influence on fear, and knowing that nothing is hiding under your bed doesn't make you any less afraid of monsters in the dark, especially when you're a child – a child suffering from SAD – and your monster lurking in the dark is the fear that something bad will happen to you or your parents whenever you're apart from each other.

If you pause to really empathize with that fear, you will see that anxiety sucks. It is terrible. It lies. It fills your head – or rather, your child's head – with doubts, and it paints an image in their minds that is the answer to this very question: What is the worst thing that can happen?

For some of them – the ones dealing with a specific phobia – the answer to that question is spiders. Or rats. Or thunderstorms. Or fire. Or needles. Or blood.

For those dealing with social anxiety disorder (or social phobia), the answer is a playgroup, or recess, or school, or having to give a speech in class…or just having to say a simple "hello" to the new neighbor's child.

For the child dealing with selective mutism, the answer to that question could be having to speak to strangers when all the words just seem to stick to their throat. And like the children suffering from social phobia, children with selective mutism may be termed "painfully shy" or "reserved." Those could be labels that they may later feel pressured to live up to, particularly when they start getting over their anxiety and someone with authority – like a teacher – comes up to them and says, "Oh, you've changed. You were rather quiet before."

The child suffering from panic disorder may find that question a bit harder to answer; in some cases, their object of anxiety may be a loss of control, and it might even be the panic itself.

And for the child suffering from generalized anxiety disorder, the answer to that question is simply: Everything.

But how do you handle all of this? And what does it mean for you, the parent of a child who is suffering from anxiety?

The simple answer is that it makes your parenting job a lot more challenging. At first, you might be thinking that this is just a phase in your child's life, and by all means, there is no reason why it can't and won't be just that. But as time goes by and you seek – or you've sought – medical help for them, and you begin the process of treating or "managing" their anxiety, reality begins to set in.

So, you start making sure that they're not in contact with the object of their anxiety. You devise coping methods and techniques that will help calm them whenever their anxiety begins to set in. That's all good and fine (and honestly, it's something that their psychologist will likely recommend). If it is extreme, you may find yourself restructuring your entire life around it – the anxiety, not your child – because you'll be doing everything within your power to prevent meltdowns and full-blown panic attack episodes.

If you're not careful, this is when you'll begin to stretch yourself thin and wear yourself out. You may find yourself doing strange things to keep your child away from the object of their anxiety.

You may even start to adjust your hopes and expectations for the child. "It's fine if Georgie doesn't want to go to school," you may say to your spouse as you are lying in bed at the end of a particularly difficult day. "He shouldn't have to be away from home if he doesn't want to. We'll just go right ahead and homeschool him. There is a pandemic, anyway."

In the same vein, you may not be as strict with them as you are with your other children because you don't want to stress them out. And you may become very lenient with them when they misbehave or bring home bad grades in their midterms. In most cases, when they misbehave, they won't even have to explain themselves because you won't give them the chance. You'll just skip right into making excuses for them.

So, instead of parenting them, you may begin to manage them and make excuses for them. And this right here is one of the greatest errors you can make when parenting a child with anxiety. The only parenting mistake that supersedes it is when you do the exact opposite, and you become too hard on your anxious child because of certain symptoms which can be perceived as inadequacies. In this particular case, you will only be adding to their anxiety, and their disorder may – and likely will – worsen as time progresses.

"Why?" You may ask. After all, you've raised children before, and all your anxious child's siblings are doing just fine.

You see, dear parent, there is no real formula to parenting. There is no magic equation or one-size-fits-all formula, but statistical bodies of evidence suggest children will do much better in a balanced environment, particularly when they suffer from anxiety. Of course, you have to shower them with love. You must give your child safety, structure, routine, and all the TLC (tender, loving care) that you have to offer as their caregiver. This is your primary duty as a parent, after all, to be the nest for your little baby bird. But do not clip their wings.

As a parent, you must raise your anxious child right. Aside from the fact that this is your moral, legal, genetic and religious obligation, you must also remember that they exist in a society that will make its demands on them when they become adults. Your anxious child has just about the same responsibilities that your non-anxious one has, and you will be doing them, yourself, society, and the world at large, a great disservice if you do not prepare them well for those responsibilities. However, you must do so properly.

So, Georgie – from our previous example – should go to school if he can. That is if his anxiety is not extreme and, his psychologist has recommended that he should. If Georgie misbehaves, he should have to explain himself, and if his explanations don't come up to scratch, well...then, he should be punished reasonably and accordingly.

Simply put, you should not coddle your anxious child in the name of "managing" them. You should actually help them. Talk to them, not for them, in the face of bad behavior, except your aim is to de-escalate an uncomfortable situation for them (in which case, you would be helping them). You must also take care not to become their drill-sergeant or the parent who goes to the extreme while you try to apply all this brilliant advice.

Ask them how they feel, hear them out, and actually listen to their fears – no matter how unwarranted or unreasonable they may be – and you must do so calmly. But you must be patient with them and with yourself. And there is another very important reason for this.

The lesser-known truth about anxiety is that it is catching, and a child can catch anxiety from their anxious parent just as easily as a parent can get it from their anxious child. If you don't believe me, think back to your child's last panic attack. Remember how you felt, how worried you were, and how afraid. Also, if your anxious child has a specific phobia for spiders and you've spent the last several months trying to keep the spiders away, try to think back to the last time you were apart from that child...and you saw a spider. Do you believe me now?

Many people will begin to worry after the Eureka moment fades that their child's anxiety might somehow be their fault, but the only thing I will say to that – for now – is that different people will react differently in uncomfortable situations. In the next chapter, we will discuss the causes of anxiety, but for now, I will focus on you, the parent of an anxious child.

So far, I've told you about anxiety. I've painted the picture for you in several shades to suit each one of the 6 major types, and I have tried to make you see things from your anxious child's point of view. I have also given you parenting advice, and I'm sure that over the course of the last several paragraphs, I have made you question –or at least wonder – about your parenting skills and consider whether or not you may be in any way responsible for your child's anxiety. I'm also sure that you're probably holding your breath, wondering what else I'm going to say next.

Well, here it is, the final point I'm going to make in this chapter: You need to take care of your own mental health. I bet you were not expecting that.

Parenting itself is an exercise – a journey – that often appears as though it is specially designed to make you question yourself. Oftentimes, you may fall into a continuous loop of entertaining "what ifs." What if you didn't do this or that? What if you insist that Georgie must go to school? What if you don't insist that Georgie must go to school? And when you have an anxious child, it doesn't get any easier.

I've said it before in a previous paragraph that a parent can catch anxiety from their child, and I'm reiterating it. Anxiety is catching. So, as you parent your anxious child, take the time to care for yourself, for your own mental health.

Caring for your anxious child can be very...testing on various levels – physically and emotionally – but you must not forget that anxiety itself exists on a very mental level. It exists mainly in the mind as uncontrolled fear, a wildfire of fear and doubt, in your anxious child's life. And fire, too, is catching. If you don't take care of yourself – particularly your own mental health – instead of serving the function of cool and calm waters, you may end up as wood in the face of the raging flames. Oh, it may take several months or years, but the stress will tell eventually. So, dear parent, do not neglect yourself.

Be calm, meditate (remember that that is the second step of how to use this book), and find the time to rest. There are excellent and credible support groups for parents of children with anxiety. If there aren't any in your vicinity, you can look into putting together one with other parents with anxious children. Whenever you feel that you also must see a psychologist, do not hesitate to do so.

Be good to yourself. Your child's treatment plan – and very possibly recovery, or at least improvement – depends heavily on the state of your own mental health.

Chapter 3:
What Are The Causes of Anxiety in Children?

Child anxiety is a very complex thing. The condition is not always easy to diagnose in children because it can present itself in various forms. Even after it has been adequately identified, it is not always easy to work out the perfect treatment plan. Child psychologists will proffer the best possible unique strategies for treating your child, and they will implement some changes as time progresses. However, one of the most essential steps in treating an anxious child is first determining the underlying cause of their anxiety. And this is perhaps one of the most important things that a child psychologist will try to unearth from their first interaction with the child.

After all, it is one thing to continually treat symptoms – like panic attacks, irrational fear of spiders, or selective mutism – as they arise and a completely different thing to discover the root of the matter and try to solve the problem from its source.
This process may prove difficult as there are many causes for anxiety in children, and two or more of them are usually present in an anxious child's life at any point in time.

Also, no matter how protective you are as a parent, or how much you try to shield them from the outside world, your children will experience things when they are apart from you; either in play, as they have fun with their mates in school or in other settings. We've established that it is your duty as a parent to prepare your children for all those life experiences and the feelings that come with them so that they will become functional and independent members of society when they become adults (even as you provide them with a safe haven at home, and in their relationship with you and other members of their family). However, some of the things that your children will experience in life – with or without you – have the potential to shake them, destroy their confidence or even traumatize them, thus resulting in anxiety.

But by first identifying the root cause of anxiety in your child's life, you can begin to help them. This is a nonnegotiable part of trying to help your child overcome their anxiety.

The most common factors that can cause anxiety in children are:
- Emotional and mental stress involved in moving houses constantly.
- Emotional strain of separation or divorce between parents, or the subsequent remarriage of one or both parents.
- Genetics or family factor comes into play due to having parents, grandparents, or other relatives with anxiety; and inheriting it from them (like eye color and the increased risk of diabetics).
- Environmental factor of being raised by parents or caregivers who have anxiety. Living with a sibling or someone with anxiety can also lead to child anxiety.
- Bullying.
- Physical, mental, or emotional abuse.

- The strain of losing a loved one and many others.

Ultimately, all these factors can be divided into three major categories, which are:
- **The biological factor**

The imbalance of certain chemical compounds or neurotransmitters in the brain may lead to anxiety in children.

Neurotransmitters are chemicals responsible for delivering messages from one part to another within the central nervous system, which includes the brain. Some of them may lead to anxiety in a child, whenever they are too much or too little.

To understand this better, we are going to imagine a little scenario. Try to imagine that you are stuck in a very important meeting at work, and then it suddenly occurs to you that you left the house with the cooker on, except that this is one of those times that you are not actually sure whether you switched it off or not. And instead of focusing on your meeting, your mind keeps racing back to the cooker. "Did I turn it off or not?" That is the thought circling around in your head. Your mind may go a little further and paint images of various scenarios involving that cooker. One minute, you're worried that the smoke will trigger the fire alarm, and in the next breath, you're scared that your entire house will go up in flames because of that carelessness (that may or may not exist).

Suddenly it occurs to you that your partner is still at home, but you're not sure that they'll remember to check the cooker before they leave the house. So, what do you do?

You pick up your phone in the middle of your very important meeting and send them a text. However, what happens when they don't reply and the seconds tick off into minutes?

Let us assume you send them another text. Maybe they still don't reply, and you keep sending texts— over and over again.

Unbeknownst to you, however, your partner is experiencing some trouble with their phone, and while they can read your texts, they can't get back to you, and to top it off, they've also – somehow – managed to lock themselves out of the house. So, they also cannot check if the cooker is on or off anyway.

Can you imagine the feelings of panic and helplessness that you and your partner would be experiencing in that moment?

Well...that situation is only an analogy for what happens in an anxious child's brain when a chemical neurotransmitter is overactive.

In that case, it will keep on sending the same message of urgency to the receiving end – which is another part of the child's brain – thus bombarding the child with feelings of anxiety that they cannot shake off.

It is a very annoying scenario, to say the least, and that feeling of helpless urgency can lead to episodes of panic attacks.

The main neurotransmitters that fall under this category are dopamine, norepinephrine, and serotonin. This is why a psychologist may recommend certain tests for the child. Some of the medication prescribed may contain precursors – or inhibitors – for one or both of these chemicals.

Many studies also show that anxious people – and children – may be more sensitive to the uptake of chemicals like lactic acid produced naturally by the muscles during physical activity. As a matter of fact, science has proven that panic attacks can be triggered in an anxious person (or child) by injecting lactic acid into their body. People with panic disorder will also have an increased risk of experiencing panic attacks whenever they breathe air with elevated levels of carbon dioxide.

The intake of substances like alcohol, nicotine, and caffeine can also trigger episodes in an anxious person. Luckily, many of these items are substances that children are not – and should not be – exposed to anyway. Still, extra care should be taken to keep the child away from these things because of their condition. If the anxious child is mature enough to want to experiment with these chemicals, the parent must impress on them exactly how harmful they are.

Although there are many studies and evidence that support these biochemical factors as a major cause of anxiety, a lot of important research is still being conducted on this area. Many unknown and unproved theories are still being investigated. Yet, the little that is known about these biological factors have proved useful over the years, particularly in the noted effectiveness of prescribed medications such as antidepressants and neurotransmitter inhibitors in the treatment of child anxiety, in some instances.

- **Genetics or family factor**

Genetics is a beautiful thing. It is the branch of science dedicated to the study of living things in respect to traits inherited from parents and ancestors, traits passed down through genes; like skin color, hair color, hair texture, the shape of their toenails, the length of their fingers, eye color, allergies and – some would even say – skill or dexterity in certain areas, subjects or instruments.

Scientists in this field have discovered that parents who suffer from anxiety – or parents who have suffered from childhood anxiety themselves – have a much greater risk of producing children with anxiety, whether these children live with them or not. This occurs much the same way that hair color, the shape of a child's nose, and the increased risk of diabetes get passed down from parent to child. And really, it isn't all that surprising, is it?

Science has always sought answers to many questions, and it has always delved into the reasons behind health disorders such as anxiety. The discovery of this link that exists between the condition and the field of genetics is truly remarkable.

That is because, in this case, genetics has provided a seemingly simple answer to the question, "Why could this be happening to my child?"

And although this answer may not cover all the reasons behind the child's anxiety, it does shed some light on the child's unique condition.

It is undeniable that genetics plays a vital role in the development of child anxiety by increasing the risk of anxiety in the children of anxious parents. And while this tendency is great, it does not mean that children of parents with anxiety – or children of parents who have suffered from anxiety in the past – will definitely manifest the same condition. It only means that they have much higher odds of developing some form of the disorder at some point in their lives, and this period could turn out to be their childhood.

The exact point in time when this condition could manifest has nothing to do with the child's choice, but it has everything to do with the presence of other internal and external factors, of which gene may only be dominant.

One would think that the science behind the inheritance of anxiety through genetics would be much clearer or more predictable in this current day and age. However, research is still ongoing about this issue. And there is still so much that scientists have not yet uncovered; though, there is undeniable evidence from various studies that prove that this inheritance and increased risk does, in fact, happen.

Much research is still underway, and scientists are trying to obtain every bit of information about this phenomenon, particularly those pertaining to the exact genetic markers responsible for anxiety – and child anxiety – as an inheritable trait.

Consequently, child anxiety may become treatable with gene therapy, both in anxious children and in the growing fetuses of parents with anxiety. Someday, in the future, this may be fully and successfully achieved. And who knows? Gene therapy might just be the cure to child anxiety. Can you imagine what this would mean for the rate of child anxiety when that time comes?

In the next decade or so, we just might see.

- **Environmental factor**

This final division of the causes of anxiety in children encompasses everything else, everything that hasn't already been covered by the biological factor and the genetics (or family factor).

That's right, we are talking about things like; the emotional and mental stress involved in moving houses constantly, the emotional strain of separation or divorce between parents (or the subsequent remarriage one of one or both parents), the "nurture factor" of being raised by parents or caregivers who have anxiety (or along with a close sibling or someone with anxiety), bullying, physical, mental or emotional abuse, the strain of losing a loved one, and many others.

Basically, this category covers anything, occurrence, or event that may create trauma or shock a child, thereby leaving a lasting effect on them, eventually developing into anxiety.

For instance, an anxious child suffering from separation anxiety disorder may have recently lost a pet or a loved one; they might have passed on or moved away suddenly, they might have even gone missing. Sometimes, it may not even be a living thing. The child may have misplaced a precious item that holds sentimental value for them, something that holds a lot of meaning to them, something that they miss. These kinds of events may cause emotional stress to the anxious child, leading to anxiety; or at least, events like this may be among the main root causes of anxiety in the child's life.

A child who experiences specific phobia may have had an early encounter with the object of their fear or anxiety that did not go very well, and this event may have left a profound imprint on their minds. However, do not lose hope yet, dear parent; no matter what that object is that your anxious child fear, it is possible for them to overcome their anxiety.

In the same vein, a child suffering from selective mutism may have had a bad experience in social situations, or they might have observed something similar happening to somebody else. But in many cases, the true origins of their condition may be deeper than that or just...different. Some children stop speaking to strangers after losing a loved one or after they have experienced some sort of trauma, bullying, abuse, or neglect. And for others, the reasons behind their anxiety disorder may not be as easy to identify. Sometimes, the child may work themselves into a state of extreme and silent anxiety whenever they find themselves in situations where they have to interact with strangers or people that they are not comfortable with for seemingly no reason. They may even tell you that they "don't know" the reason themselves. As a parent, don't let this get you down. Don't let yourself be frustrated. Simply try to help your child as much as you can.

The same things may hold true for children with social anxiety disorder (or social phobia), panic disorder, and generalized anxiety disorder (GAD).
As we come to the close of this chapter, I would like to encourage you again, dear parent, to remain strong.
The process of uncovering the true causes of your child's anxiety may prove difficult and traumatizing – even to you – because you may end up finding out things that you are not fully equipped to deal with. After all, whatever thing, situation, or tragic event that has led to the development of such a disorder in your child's life will certainly not bring you joy. And even when those underlying reasons seem so easily identifiable, that doesn't necessarily mean that they are easier to deal with. This is why, at this stage in your child's treatment, you need to stand your ground against frustration. You must be patient, and you must be ready to listen to your child's psychologist.

However, do not hesitate to seek a second professional opinion if you feel the need to. And as you do all you can to help your child, remember to take care of yourself.

Chapter 4:
What Could Possibly Happen To Your Child If You Don't Do Anything?

When a child develops an anxiety disorder, it can be tough for all persons involved. The child won't have an easy time of it, nor will the parents (or siblings, for that matter); and a big reason for all of this is that anxiety usually comes into a person's life with all its bags and baggage ready to be unpacked. It will find a choice place for itself in the individual's head and life, and it will make itself right at home. Even when that individual is a child, this disorder will be fully prepared to last forever. The good old "let's-do-nothing-but-hope-they-outgrow-it" method is not likely to work here. In fact, most of the time, anxiety will withstand whatever you throw at it. It will not be easily reasoned with or dealt with. And though this disorder may sometimes be harder to handle in children than in adults, treatment could be a lot more rewarding.

Children may be more likely to overcome their fears and anxiety than adults because of their inherent resilience. Following this, they can chalk it all up to childhood silliness, if they so wish. Be that as it may, however, anxiety must still be addressed and treated in the child. Because even in the best-case scenarios, after he or she has been "cured," they may still have lingering feelings that panic attacks are waiting at every corner. And in the worst cases, when the child's anxiety is entirely ignored by their parents and caregivers, many things are likely to happen. What you should know is that, in most cases, the child will eventually come up with their own way of dealing with their disorder, however effective or ineffective that method might be.

We have already established, in previous chapters, that anxiety can bleed into other areas of the child's life (as well as other people's lives) but can this disorder continue to influence the child's emotions and behaviors all the way into adulthood?

The simple answer is "Yes."

In the instance of the child with separation anxiety disorder, they may grow up completely unable to be apart from their parents and caregivers – or whoever else is the object of their anxiety – for too long. This means that they may never move out of their parents' homes, not because they are broke or unemployed or because they have no need for their own space, but because they have never quite been able to stop being restless or gotten over the feeling that "something bad" is going to happen if they spend too much time apart from their parents and caregivers (or whoever else is the object of their anxiety).

This debilitating fear may follow them well into adulthood. Then, when they become parents, their separation anxiety disorder may morph into a fear of being apart from their own children. This disorder may also influence the child's other relationships later in life. As adults, their friends and acquaintances may find them "too clingy," as they may be afraid of being alone. I do not have to go into all the details of how this could end up very badly for the anxious child turned adult. Too many things could happen; they may end up with narcissistic partners or egoists who thrive on that kind of attention without knowing the true cause. They may end up passing up life-changing opportunities because of that terrible fear, and ultimately, they may end up with bad experiences in life...all because of unresolved childhood anxiety.

Conversely, the child with a specific phobia may develop an extreme fear of the target of their anxiety. They may end up as adults who build their whole lives around that anxiety. It may influence where they live, what kind of career path they take, the kind of choices they make, and so on. As a matter of fact, some of these anxious children – turned adults –may end up exhibiting signs of other types of phobia such as agoraphobia (the extreme fear of open spaces or of going outside) and other antisocial behaviors, which they think may keep them apart from the object of their specific anxiety. If this kind of behavior continues unchecked for several years, it may largely impair the child's life, as well as the quality of life in terms of meaningful relationships and experiences; negatively influencing their careers, associations, and basically everything else about them, all of which may have been avoided if their parents and caregivers had gotten appropriate help for their child's anxiety disorder when they were young.

Similarly, the child with unaddressed and untreated selective mutism may never learn to speak up in front of others. Such children may grow up to be adults who cannot express themselves before people, at work or elsewhere, that they are not comfortable with. And it won't necessarily be because they do not know what to say and how to say it, but because they simply cannot get all the words out. Sometimes, they may even be averse to other communication forms during these periods because the panic inherent in these episodes may not allow them to be articulate enough to write down or sign out how they feel.

This disorder may eat so deeply into their lives as adults that it will create a façade of unshakable meekness that really isn't their nature, thus resulting in a sort of double life where people know them to be one thing outside, but they are entirely different when they are with their loved ones at home; charismatic, confident and warm. Such a situation may make things difficult for this child — turned adult— in the labor market and in the workforce. And they may get passed up for promotions at their jobs because they are perceived as not confident enough or too shy or timid. Others may take credit for their work in such situations and even make a habit of it when they feel that they can easily get away with it. Now, these are all speculations, but quite simply put, a child with selective mutism or an adult with this disorder is easy prey in our kind of world, where evil exists alongside the good, and a person's voice is such a precious thing. Selective mutism goes far beyond not being able to string together words during panic attacks; it is a robbery of your child's ability to speak out. And if for nothing else but this reason, you must get your child all the help they need when this disorder presents itself in their lives.

Similarly, a child with social anxiety disorder may have difficulty blending into society as an adult, most especially if their anxiety was not addressed or treated during childhood. Children like this may likely grow up to be antisocial or asocial in one form or another as a way of dealing with the feelings they get around strangers or in uncomfortable social situations. They may isolate themselves from society and become hermits, not out of choice, but because they want to avoid episodes of panic attacks. They may underperform in school or at work because they do not want to be the focus of attention. And because of the child – turned adult's –perceived meekness may also become easy targets of people with narcissistic tendencies. These kinds of people will feel like the child – turned adult –can be easily controlled and managed. Because they are not likely to have many friends, the narcissist may easily presume that their toxic activities will continue unchecked for quite a while. Now, these assumptions may be entirely unfounded, but narcissists may not care until they have had a very rude awakening, a situation that the child – turned adult –may have completely avoided if things had been much different and their anxiety disorder had been treated during childhood. There are mere speculations. The reality of untreated social phobia in a child may turn out to be much worse or better, in extreme instances – but there is no doubt that proper treatment of anxiety disorder will make a wealth of difference in the child's life.

Much the same way, untreated panic disorder may be debilitating for children when they become adults. As a matter of fact, the effects of panic disorder – and other forms of child anxiety – won't just show up when the child becomes an adult. This form of childhood anxiety disorder and other forms may trail the anxious child from childhood, through puberty and adolescence, into adulthood, thus leaving its terrible taint on the child's entire life. Of course, there will be good times, but there will also be bad times. And many of those bad times will feature the child, teenager, or adult suffering from extreme fear, shortness of breath, increased heart rate, nausea, dizziness, shaky and clammy hands, headaches, chest pains, and every other symptom that constitutes a panic attack. Now, this is all just speculation, and maybe the child will "get over it," which is the end goal of the classic "let's-do-nothing-but-hope-they-outgrow-it" approach. But the odds are that they may not be able to overcome this disorder on their own. That they may pass out from panic attacks more than a couple times on the road between childhood and adulthood, and that even when they finally become adults, their disorder may remain, or it could have worsened. But what if you take a different approach as their parent and caregiver? What if you get them some help for their anxiety while they are still in their childhood?   How might that make a difference?

A child with generalized anxiety disorder may grow up being afraid of everything in the world. The minds of children like this are always filled with disasters waiting to happen at every turn. And if they don't get all the help they need as children, they may grow up to be adults who worry about everything. And because the brains of anxious people under this category are constantly at work, worrying over every instance of "impending doom," they may not have enough energy or attention to focus on anything else. They may not be able to function at school or make deadlines at work. Basically, they may become adults whose whole worlds revolve around possibilities of disasters that may never actually happen. But for them, that possibility, no matter how slim it is, is everything. Children like this may not know how to stop obsessing over every little thing that might go wrong and just enjoy all their moments, and as adults with responsibilities, they may become worse. But when this childhood anxiety disorder is detected early by the parents and caregivers of the anxious child – and it is immediately addressed – the child has a much better prognosis and considerably higher chances of beating this psychological disorder.

The role of a parent or caregiver does not end there. In addition to therapy and other medical care, which may have been recommended by their child's psychologist in the treatment of their specific anxiety disorder, the parents must take an active role in their child's treatment.

You must monitor your child's progress in dealing with their anxiety as time passes, and you must pay attention. As you do all of this and more, you must also keep in mind that the goal of treating your child's anxiety is not only to "manage" but to help them "overcome."

"What is the difference?" You may ask.

As discussed previously, when we set out to "manage" a disorder like anxiety or even think about it in simple conversational terms, we tend to set minimal expectations for ourselves (as parents) and the child. We may become unnecessarily content with very little progress, as long as what they (the anxious child) are feeling isn't too overwhelming, they are functional, and their anxiety isn't crippling. When, in fact, we ought to see this progress – this success in "managing" their anxiety – as a milestone, knowing full well or at least having hope that there may still be a lot of progress to achieve…that right there, well, that is the "overcoming" spirit.

I mentioned earlier that treating anxiety in children can be very rewarding because children are resilient, but perhaps, I wasn't clear enough in my reasoning. Young children are fearless by nature. They are not designed to be fearful creatures. And even the timidest of them will shock you with cheekiness on occasion. Their minds are still collecting information on the rest of the world, you see. So, how can they fear the unknown? Why should they? It is we adults that mince words and hide our feeling, even as we fear the things that we do not know. Once you can look beyond their fear of monsters hiding under their beds, it becomes easier to see that children are immensely brave. After all, they are themselves, aren't they? They don't hang up their true natures in dark closets behind many walls. With many of them, what you see is exactly what you get. And if that is not the true definition of bravery, then what is?

As you consider that, I would also like you to ask yourself these questions: "Why should you settle for less?" "Why should you be satisfied with very little progress when your child may be capable of more?" "Why should your goal be the 'management' of your anxious child's anxiety, rather than its 'cure'?"

A lot of children will spend the rest of their lives "managing" their childhood anxiety disorder and living with it because as soon as they were able to handle themselves during episodes of panic attacks, their parents sighed deeply and thought to themselves, "Ha! Our job here is done." However, there are children who go on to live their lives without the shadow of those anxieties hanging over them. And while your child's success in overcoming their disorder does not rest solely on you – no matter what you do – you do have a key role to play in their treatment as their parent or caregiver. There may be no "cure" yet for anxiety, but child anxiety can be overcome, and you will be doing yours a great disservice by settling for less.

Having said this, you do not necessarily need to transform into their drill sergeant. You only have to continue parenting them, caring for them, and keeping a close eye on their progress.

Make no mistake; your child's success in "managing" their anxiety disorder is not a bad thing. As a matter of fact, it is a wonderful thing. It is a milestone. It is a crest of treatment and a sign that all the care you have given to them is finally paying off during this trying time. But it may only be the beginning, so please, do not be in a hurry to discontinue treatment as soon as it starts paying off.

Chapter 5:
What You Can Do To Help Your Child Overcome His Anxiety

The first thing you can do to help your anxious child overcome their anxiety is to pay close attention to them. You must take care to notice your child's habits and behaviors and deduce their reasons for doing the things they do and acting the way they do. Most especially, you must take care to observe what they avoid and how they interact with those things when they seem to have no choice in the issue. Sometimes, the things they go out of their way to avoid may not actually be things; it could be certain situations like any form of separation from their parents or caregivers or even the presence of strangers.

These symptoms are not always easy to notice, but they are glaring in others. For instance, children with separation anxiety disorder may throw tantrums whenever they are about to be apart from their parents. They may also cry and exhibit signs of restlessness whenever until their parents or caregivers return to them. But, while this behavior is common among very young children, children with separation anxiety disorder may also exhibit a noticeable amount of terror along with their tantrums. This terror or extreme fear of separation in the child usually doesn't abate with time, and it is a real and visceral thing; a genuine and nearly unshakable fear that has gained ground in their heart and mind, drowning out all rational thought pertaining to the true nature of their parents' or caregiver's absence. Other symptoms of this terrible disorder include increased heart rate, sweaty palms, tangible and almost paralyzing terror at their parent's absence, and an unshakable belief that "something bad" is going to happen.

Conversely, a specific phobia may be hard to detect in an anxious child; particularly if that child is generally reserved by nature, or they do not feel the need to share their fear of the object of their anxiety or – most likely – they simply do not wish to talk about it, because then, their feelings of anxiety would become all too real. With some children, it is an issue of bravery; they may feel as if admitting their extreme anxiety over a specific object will make people see them as childish. This may be the case with children from age 7 and above or children in their preteens, who are logical enough to know that they shouldn't be afraid of the specific object of their anxiety but fear it anyway. These children may even prove harder to help in terms of getting them psychological treatment because of the extra walls and reservations that they have erected around themselves. However, in instances where specific phobia is easily detected, parents and caregivers should be careful not to upset the child further by being insensitive to the object of their specific phobia. Be it clowns or spiders, storms, tight spaces, or even buttons, the anxious child's phobia should be acknowledged, respected, and taken into consideration (as well as taken seriously). As an anxious child's parent or caregiver, you must keep in mind that a phobia – by definition – is an extreme and irrational fear. That fear isn't likely to go away just because you tell your child to "chin up" or "stop being a baby." You need to first talk to them about it, seek psychological help for them as deemed necessary by the medical experts, and shower them with tender loving care and a great deal of patience.

Likewise, the symptoms of selective mutism may be hard to detect in some children; though, this is not usually the case. As a matter of fact, the symptoms of selective mutism are usually very noticeable, the most common of which is the child's unwillingness or near inability to talk under certain circumstances. However, the reasons for this disorder may not be as easily deduced, as the child may exhibit a tendency to clam up whenever the issue is broached. It is, however, imperative to know – as a parent or caregiver to such a child – that you must continue to ask the right questions, and you must do so gently. You must also be patient with your child during this period. Remember, dear parent, the cause of the child's selective mutism – in this instance – is anxiety, so it will only be adding to the anxious child's tumultuous feelings if you lose your temper or raise your voice in an attempt to get them to speak. This approach may worsen their disorder, and it may also result in the development of other forms of anxiety such as panic disorder.

Social anxiety disorder or social phobia may go undetected for some time; since it can be easily confused for a child's natural tendency to be reserved or quiet in some cases. However, like with other forms of anxiety, the telltale symptom that will confirm that the child's behavior is indeed a result of social phobia is the inherent anxiety or extreme fear that may be glaringly obvious in their symptoms and behavior. The parents of a child with social anxiety disorder and of those exhibiting symptoms of other forms of anxiety must also endeavor to speak with their child's teachers at school. Make enquires and ask questions like: "How does Georgie (replace 'Georgie' with your anxious child's name) behave at school?" "How does he react whenever he is called upon to answer questions in class?" "How does he act around his peers?" And then, you must listen to what the teachers have to say about your anxious child's behavior and add their observations to your findings.

Another thing you may have to do is to hear from the child's very close friends. You may find subtle ways to make your inquiries (to avoid any situation that your child may constitute as a breach of trust, especially if they are around 9 years of age or older). In fact, to stay on the safer side of things, you may first want to ask these close friends' parents if their child has said anything of concern about yours. Hear what they have to say and add it to your list of findings. Then, try to piece together all the information.

On the other hand, a child with panic disorder may have already experienced their first few episodes before their parents or caregivers become aware of the disorder. However, a common symptom of this disorder – aside from anxiety – is the inherent fear of more anxiety attacks. The child may exhibit signs of extreme fear in certain situations, particularly when they begin to feel overwhelmed. They may also try to excuse themselves whenever they perceive the onslaught of symptoms like increased heart rates, headaches, nausea or queasiness, clammy or sweaty palms, constricted throat or difficulty in breathing, and other telltale signs of an impending panic attack episode. Unfortunately, one episode of panic attack, though alarming, does not necessarily indicate a panic disorder, and while you are still observing your child and gathering findings on their anxious behavior, this disorder may worsen.

For this reason, you must make haste as soon as you detect these symptoms or as soon as you witness their first panic attack (which may not actually be their first episode, in any case). Ask them relevant questions, and set about seeking medical and psychological help for them. The sooner you do this for your child, the better for all parties involved and the more rewarding, as far as the efficacy of treatment is concerned.

In the case of general anxiety disorder, this form of anxiety may be one of the easiest to notice. However, it may still be hard for the child's parents and caregivers to correctly interpret their symptoms. This form of anxiety may eat so deep into the child's life that their parents and caregivers may wrongfully ascribe it to their personality. That is when you, as a parent, become so used to your child's anxious behavior that you may even be found saying things like, "Oh, that's just how Georgie (replace this name with that of the anxious child) is. He's a very careful sort, that boy." You may even begin to see some of their symptoms as an early indication of anxiety when, in fact, that may not be the case.

One important thing you should bear in mind is that anxiety may often present itself in more than one way in the child's life, and so, a child with selective mutism may also develop a social phobia or social anxiety disorder; the underlying reason being a certain fear of speaking to or seeing. Following this theory, it becomes quite easy to see how a child with general anxiety disorder may develop specific phobia, separation anxiety disorder, or even some forms of OCD (obsessive-compulsive disorder) in a bid to gain some control over the unyielding anxiety battering at their mind.

In an earlier chapter, we likened the predicament of the child suffering from GAD to that of the myth god, Atlas, with the weight of the world on their shoulders. Dear parent, do not mistake your child's anxiety for responsibility or caution because neither of those things involves extreme or debilitating fear and all the symptoms of panic attacks or other anxiety disorders. GAD is a disorder, and it must be treated as such, even in its earliest phases.

Some of the questions that parents and caregivers must ask themselves to help them detect real symptoms of anxiety disorders as they observe the habits of their anxious child are:
- "Is there a specific object or situation that my child goes out of their way to avoid?"

- "Do they throw tantrums whenever they have to be away from my partner and me?" And if the answer to this question is "Yes," you need to ask yourself a follow-up question: "Have they lost anybody or anything important to them recently?"
- "Do they freeze up whenever they have to speak to unfamiliar people?"
- "Is my child entirely too quiet around outsiders, contrary to their bubbly personality at home?"
- "Does my child display an undue amount of worry or stress over things that they cannot control, some of which are extremely unlikely to happen?"
- "Does my child avoid certain things because they don't like them, or is there a deeper reason behind their behavior?"
- "And if there is a deeper reason, could it be extreme fear or anxiety?"
- "Do they get panic attacks?" And if so, "How often do they get panic attacks?"

You must be honest with yourself as you answer those questions, and you must also be as objective as possible in your observations. Remember, it wouldn't do your child any good if you make excuses for them or to try and rationalize their habits, especially when those behaviors fit right in with symptoms of anxiety disorders (which have already been identified and discussed earlier in this chapter, as well as in previous ones).

You must also exercise care and prudence in your interpretation of your child's behavior because some forms of anxiety can be harder to detect than others, especially when they first begin to manifest. On the other hand, sometimes, the child's anxiety may be normal, and their symptoms may not be due to an anxiety disorder at all; in this case, that fear may fade with time.

However, once any symptom of anxiety is detected in your child's behavior, you must pay close attention to them. Speak to them about it and ask them questions like:
- "What is wrong?"
- "Why don't you want to leave Mommy and Daddy?"
- "Do you think the storm (or whatever the object of their specific phobia is) is scary?"
- "Does (insert whatever thing or situation you notice them avoiding) scare you?"
- "Don't you want to play with your friends?" (That is in the instance where the child isolates themselves from others)

And so on.

Listen to their answers and try to empathize. Endeavor to talk it out with them and do so gently, with utmost care. However, if these symptoms begin to pile up over time, along with tell-tale signs like shortness of breath, extreme terror or fear, constant bouts of crying and tantrums, increased heart rate, sweaty and clammy hands, selective mutism, increased or noticeable lack of confidence and constant worrying, among others, then your child may have an anxiety disorder. As soon as you realize this, you must seek psychological help for them.

Child psychologists are the experts when it comes to the treatment of your child's anxiety. You can find them at your nearest hospital or look them up on certified sites online. (Though the hospital route might be the best way to go). And if your observations are very compelling, the first thing any proper child psychologist will do after listening to your concerns is to schedule a consultation with your child. Your observations, along with the psychologist's assessment of your child, will form the basis of your child's unique diagnosis. And if your child is diagnosed with an anxiety disorder...well then, don't be discouraged. It is all a part of the process.

Following your child's diagnosis, the psychologist will deliver their prognosis, which is basically an evaluation of the child's probability of overcoming their anxiety. This probability is usually higher for children than for adults (because of their innate resilience, remember). And then, they will form a treatment plan. This usually includes scheduled hours for therapy, meditation, and a lot of mental and emotional exercises for both parent and child. In some cases, medication may even be prescribed.

As a parent or caregiver, you need to be in full cooperation with the child psychologist. And they must be willing to work with you as well. Because your child is not yet an adult, you must be privy to every detail of their sessions with the psychologist or therapist. But your responsibility as a parent or caretaker goes far beyond that. Table your own suggestions and fears to the psychologist and let them explain things to you (that is also part of their job, as the child is still a minor). Finally, you must encourage your child as they receive treatment, and you must be patient with them, even as you parent them. But most of all, you must not give up.

Chapter 6:
What You Can Say to Help Your Child Become Less Anxious

One of the most important ways to encourage your child and help them become less anxious is to say positive things. This is particularly important as the child struggles with their disorder and receives medical and psychological treatment.

Positivity is a significant factor in treating anxiety in children because it goes a long way in creating the right sort of environment for them. Quite simply, when the parents and caregivers of children with anxiety have the right outlook on things – about their child's disorder and about life in general – it can help the child become less anxious. And by creating a calm, stable, and warm social, emotional, and mental environment for them at home – a safe haven, where love, encouragement, and growth can thrive – you will also be creating the right sort of environment for them; one that will aid the effectiveness of your anxious child's medical and psychological treatment.

This is because every child requires a measure of stability in their lives, and their home is the first and most important source of it. So, when parents and caregivers make a concerted effort to provide this much-needed emotional stability for a child with anxiety – a disorder that creates mental and emotional chaos and thrives on it – it can help dispel the anxiety.

"How does this work?" You may ask.

Well, dear parent, you may recall that in earlier chapters – Chapter 2, particularly – we discussed that anxiety can be catching and that an anxious parent or caregiver may somehow transfer their own anxiety to their child through the genetic factor (or family factor), close contact or by some other means. Well, that theory also forms the basis of what has been discussed thus far in this chapter. To further clarify things, I guess we might say that children are generally sensitive people and are extraordinarily insightful. They are also known to pick up on things that most adults think they have under control. Just think about all those times you've returned home from work worn-out and tired, or upset over something that happened at work or in the parking lot or inside traffic, but right before trudging through the front door, you've pasted a convincing smile on your face and attempted to wipe your mind clean. Yet one of the first things that come out of your child's mouth when they saw you was: "What's wrong, Mommy?" or "What's wrong, Daddy?"

Or maybe you've just finished arguing with someone over the phone, and you're trying to put it out of your mind and go about your day, but then your child immediately walks up to you and gives you a hug because "you look sad."

There are a million and one examples of instances like this, when children – young children, specifically – have proven themselves to be expert barometers of human emotions, although they might not even really understand what those emotions are or why you, as a parent or caregiver (or sibling or other family members – or even stranger), are feeling that way. And that is their special magic, one of their many special gifts; that empathy. Now, a young child with an anxiety disorder has a stronger version of that; we are talking about Human Emotion Barometer 2.0, that kind that specializes in anxiety and comes with an advanced antenna that can detect that horrible feeling from miles and miles away.

For this reason, it is imperative that you create an atmosphere of positivity and stability. Not just for your child, but for you as well. When the effects of anxiety on family life are studied, it becomes quite easy, in some instances, to see how everything forms a cycle. The behavior of an anxious caregiver or parent (or close relative) may somehow influence that of the child and vice versa. And so, the parents and caregivers of the anxious child should guard their own mental wellbeing as they seek help for their anxious child. Maintaining a positive attitude is a big part of doing that. A positive disposition on the part of the child's parents or caregivers is also required for the effectiveness of encouraging words.

What all this simply means is that it is not enough for you to give verbal encouragement to your anxious child. You must also project positivity to them, even as you create the right kind of emotional and mental climate, one that is free of the added strain of your own fears, anxieties, and frustration.

In line with this, there are certain information – strategies and instances –prepared to assist you as you set about discovering answers to this big question: "What can you say to help your child become less anxious?" And as we explore this, you may also receive foundational insight into some of the things you should never say to your anxious child.

For instance, a parent or caregiver of a child with separation anxiety disorder should always explain why they have to go. Do bear in mind that this strategy will involve answering a lot of your child's questions, many of which may begin with that banal word "Why..?"

So, you may say things like: "Mommy (or Daddy) has to go to work now. Be a good boy (or girl) for (insert the name of their teacher or whoever will be responsible for them until you return)." Bear in mind that your tone of voice is very important. You must speak gently but do not waver. Going to work is something you must do; it is non-negotiable. So, when your child asks you "Why?" (As in, "Why must you go to work?"), try telling them that "All grownups have to go to work." Or "Because Mommy (or Daddy) made a commitment, and they must keep their word."

Try to be as patient and understanding as possible. Do not be short, sharp, mocking, or abrasive with them, and under no circumstances are you to burden them with words like: "Mommy (Or Daddy) must go to work because if they don't go to work, they will be fired, and we'll starve. We won't be able to pay rent, and we'll wind up homeless and living in the streets." While the core lesson of adult responsibility intrinsic in this rather explicit explanation is not a bad thing, it may only end up painting scenarios of concern in the child's mind, particularly when delivered in the wrong way.

And you may find yourself inadvertently laying the foundations or watering the seeds of general anxiety disorder in the child's life; they may start worrying about you losing your job and the entire family winding up homeless and living in the streets. It doesn't always work out that way, though, but it is best to err on the side of caution and steer clear of such explicit and negative scenes.

Instead, direct your efforts to rewarding them with something they love, something meaningful – it could be a small thing like a toy or a snack or ice-cream or a new storybook, just something – every time they behave themselves in your absence and are good to their teacher or whoever will be responsible for them until you return. Tell them that they've been good and praise them for their bravery. Such positivity is most likely to encourage more good behavior. And you'll be giving them incentives to be brave when you are apart from them. You may also want to find hobbies for them, simple tasks or educational interests that may keep them occupied in your absence, things that you may reward them for if they do a good job. This approach may also make them easier to handle for their babysitter, teacher, or caretaker until you return.

In the instance of the child with specific phobia, it is unwise to mock them with the object of their anxiety or say words like "How can you still be afraid of (insert the object of their phobia) at your age?" Or "You are no longer a baby!" "Children who are younger than you have gotten over it already; when will you?" And under no circumstances must you call them names or hurl verbal abuses at them. Never raise your hand to them, and do try to avoid raising your voice. Aside from the common and obvious detriments of some of these things (morally and legally speaking), you will only be compounding their fear and anxiety. Talk to your child and do so gently, empathize with them, be calm. If they are afraid of spiders, you can buy them fun books about spiders and other insects; not about how many eyes they have or how many eggs they lay, but about how they may sometimes aid the pollination of flowers and how not all of them are poisonous.

Nothing drives away fear quite like laughter, and nothing drives away the monsters quite like light. Make no mistake, I am not telling you to bombard your child with undesired facts about the object of their fear. I'm simply telling you to try to remove the mystery factor of that fear in the most humane way possible; this means telling them only as much as they need to know to reduce their fear. This means telling them things like: "Do you know that the spider is probably a lot more afraid of you than you are of it?" or "If you don't like clowns, you only have to look away, or you can just look at their toys." Or "Do you know that thunder actually can't hurt you?" Tell them that it is okay to be afraid, but what is not okay is allowing that fear to consume them. And if they ever ask you if you're ever afraid, do be honest with them. The goal of this exercise is not necessarily to get them to fall in love with the object of their fear or force them to interact with it, or even to get them to stop disliking it. It helps them overcome their extreme fear and anxiety to make them see that they are brave enough to deal with that thing when they must, without freezing up or losing themselves to tantrums or panic attacks. You should also do well to reward marked progress and good behavior, and when they (your anxious child) finally overcome their anxiety, do well to close that chapter behind them. You do not have to keep reminding them of their anxiety as they journey on the road to adulthood; it serves no purpose. But that doesn't mean you should stop observing them and how they behave subsequently around the object of their anxiety.

Similarly, in children with selective mutism and social anxiety disorder, you shouldn't force them to speak to people. Only do well to expose them to social situations every now and then. You should discuss the frequency of these attempts and the nature of them with their child's psychologist so that you and the medical expert can work together to help your child. This suggestion particularly comes into play as a way of preventing conflicting approaches because, in certain situations, your anxious child's psychologist may have prescribed more "one-on-one" interactions for them, after deducing that this may be all your child is ready for at that stage in their treatment, but during that period, you may be busy planning a big surprise birthday party for them. You might have sent out invitations to all their classmates, neighbors, and family members. Imagine how counter-productive or confusing that scenario may be to your child and their treatment plan.

Raising a child with selective mutism or social anxiety may be much harder for naturally bubbly and charismatic parents; in fact, raising a child with any form of anxiety may be especially taxing. Not only can it be done, but it can also be done well. Especially when you do your utmost best for your child.

Talk about their anxiety to them, listen to them, work hand in hand with their child's psychologist and them, don't make them feel bad about themselves because of what they fear or how long they have feared it, always encourage them (I really cannot stress this enough) and always try your very best to be supportive. As I said, positivity is not just about saying nice things; it is about your deeds and habits; and so, you must also work on yourself and put your time, effort, and money where your mouth is.

All of this also holds true in treating children with any form of child anxiety. Beware that many anxious children will display signs of more than one form of anxiety at some point. Ultimately, parents need to provide that air of emotional and mental stability for their anxious child and other children in their home. It is their responsibility and so much more than that. It cannot be possible until the parents or caregivers manage to sort out their own anxieties and frustrations.

Chapter 7:
Dos and Don'ts of Raising an Anxious Child (With Examples and FAQs)

The very first point I would like to make in this chapter is that anxious children or children with anxiety are still children, and so being, they are unique, young, and impressionable. And most importantly, in the course of this text, they require proper guidance and parenting.

The reason why I am reiterating this point is that anxiety disorders can place undue stress on the minds of anxious children, and when their parents and caregivers spend time observing these effects of anxiety, as well as their struggles, it can be easy to lose sight of that.

Good parents always want what is best for their children, and so, you may begin to overtly rationalize some of your anxious child's behavior or make excuses for them throughout their struggles and psychological treatment. And as time passes by, you may become too lenient with them, or the quite the contrary. In many cases, we see parents or caregivers who have become overly zealous about their children's achievements, particularly in the wake of their child's diagnosis. These parents are the sort who have chosen to see their anxious child's anxiety as a challenge issued by providence to test their parenting skills, a 100 meters race that they think will only be worn with consistent speed, agility, and grit. Now, neither of these approaches are inherently bad, after all, you are coming from a good place and have good intentions, but we cannot ignore the fatal flaws that are intrinsic in each approach. The first approach lacks discipline while the latter may be quite lacking on the finer points of patience, as far as child-rearing is concerned. What we're getting at – quite simply —is that an anxious child is a child, and as such, they have the same primary needs as any other child, as well as milestones and expectations and responsibilities both at home and in school or elsewhere.

In earlier chapters – Chapter 2, to be precise – we talked about this in terms of how children with anxiety should not be coddled because of their disorder. But they should not be pushed too hard at the same time. It is inadvisable to push them harder than they ought to be pushed at any given moment – based on the stage of treatment that they happen to be at – because you will only be adding undue, and additional, stress unto the feelings of anxiousness that they are already battling with.

In light of all of this, what then should you do? (This is our most frequently asked question or FAQ about raising a child with a form of anxiety disorder.)

Well, I've said it before in earlier chapters, and I will say it again, albeit using different words; as a parent or caregiver of an anxious child, you must strive for a balance. Try to find the perfect line between being considerate to your anxious child's needs and all the stricter sides of parenting. You must find this balance and be consistent with it. Otherwise, your child's basic needs may not be well met, the reason being that you may end up being too lax or too strict with your anxious child, because of their disorder, to the detriment of their emotional and mental wellbeing.

And so, balance is required on your part as a parent or caregiver to your child – balance and stability – so that you won't end up being too much or too little of anything.

I would like to delve deeper into the dos and don'ts of parenting a child with anxiety.

If you've been paying attention in the course of this text, then many of these points will not be new to you.

First, we shall examine the don'ts:

- **Do not raise your voice to your anxious child.**

Aside from the fact that raising your voice constantly, as a parent or caregiver, to any child (anxious or not) is not an ideal parenting strategy, this approach may serve to cultivate an anxious environment for the child. Raised voices and chaotic emotional and mental climates tend to go hand in hand, along with anger, frustration, and a whole host of other negative emotions that may only add to the anxious child's environment. For this reason, it is advisable for you – as a good parent or caregiver to the anxious child – to try your possible best to not raise your voice out of anger or otherwise.

- **Do not make a habit of losing your temper**

When your goal, as a parent or caregiver, to an anxious child is to help them beat their anxiety, you must first work on yourself. Learn to control yourself and master your temper. Avoid bouts of anger or any kind of tantrum yourself. This is because your goal is to provide the best kind of stable environment for your unique child. So in the midst of all the anxiety and chaos going on in their minds – or headspace, as the kids say – you must strive to be the calm in the eye of their storm (or anxiety disorder, if you will). You must be the insulator, a source of comfort to them like the warm blanket on a chilly day. And to do this – to be this – you must be strong and brave, you must master your temper and frustrations, and never lose sight of this, at least to the very best of your abilities. And if those abilities fall short, don't beat yourself up; instead, focus and learn how to become better for your child. To accomplish this, you yourself can sign up for anger management programs or other forms of psychological therapy.

- **Do not ignore your anxious child's emotions**

Now, you may read this and think to yourself that "Of course, I will never do this" or "No good parent will ever do this."

Well, I should probably explain further. Of course, no good parent will ever knowingly ignore their child's emotions. But you must understand that many parents often fall into the habit of misjudging the intensity of their child's emotions, particularly when that child has just been diagnosed with an anxiety disorder.

Throughout this text, we have tried to intimate parents and caregivers with the effects of anxiety and what this disorder does to an anxious child. However, except you have firsthand experience, or you can empathize really well, you may find yourself misjudging the intensity of your child's emotions on occasion. And what exactly does this mean? This means that a time will come when the strain of your child's anxiety disorder may be overwhelming, even for the most empathizing of parents. And then you may find yourself telling your anxious child to "snap out of it" or get themselves together, when in fact, they may be having a really serious anxiety episode or panic attack (or they may be standing just on the brink of one). Situations like this may end up causing a rift in the child's relationship with such parent or caregiver if it goes on for too long or it happens at a very important time or place (like in public) because the anxious child may not be able to get themselves together; in fact, their powerlessness to do so, to help themselves in moments of panic attacks, is part of what makes this disorder so serious.

So, do not ignore your child's emotions or the intensity of them. Always try to empathize with them, do not force them too far out of their comfort zone too soon, and do not hesitate to seek medical and psychological help for them as soon as you start noticing symptoms of child anxiety (This last one is of the most common mistakes that parents and caregivers of anxious children make.)

- **Do not do anything to sabotage your child's treatment plan or the efforts of their psychologist.**

As parents and caregivers to young ones, we may have our own goals, hopes, and dreams as far as our young children are concerned. Once anxiety rears its ugly head, however, it may seem as if all those expectations are already down the drain. This feeling of disappointment is very common in parents and caregivers of anxious children, and it will come at one point or the other, even if it may last only for a moment. It is a perfectly understandable feeling, and even parents and caregivers of children who have not been diagnosed with anxiety may feel the same way from time to time. I think such an emotion comes about whenever a child is doing something different from the goals, dreams, and expectations of what we may have planned out for them. While this may not necessarily be a bad thing, it can be quite frustrating to a parent or caregiver. And so, it may be tempting to want to pursue those expectations of yours, even when your child's psychologist may be recommending something much different, thus leading to situations where the child's treatment plans and the psychologist's efforts are being sabotaged.

To prevent this, I recommend that you talk to your child's psychologist about what you want for your child so that together you can work hand in hand with the child – who must also be a willing participant –to make those dreams come true.

And now, for the dos:

- **Pay attention to your child and observe their symptoms**

It is very important for parents and caregivers to pay close attention to their children. When you do this, you will notice changes in their behavior (for better or worse) a lot more quickly and easily than you would if you do not pay attention to them and observe them. Now, it is understandable that this may be a bit more difficult to do in this day and age, with work, school, the internet, and a million and one tiny distractions that may get in the way of you spending time with your child (with anxiety or without anxiety). However, it must be done, and you must make the time. Indeed, this is your responsibility as their parent or caregiver.

- **Listen to your child**

You should always take the time to ask your child gentle questions about their day and what they may be feeling in situations known to make them uncomfortable. You may ask your child with social phobia, or selective mutism questions like: "Did you learn anything interesting in class today?" And if the answer is something they are enthusiastic about, you can ask follow-up questions like, "Did your teacher ask any questions about it?" "You know the answer to that. Why didn't you raise your hand?" Try to be as gentle as possible, and when they answer your questions honestly, try to put yourself in their shoes.

- **Get them medical and psychological help as soon as possible.**

This is a very important point, and we have already emphasized it at several points throughout this book. However, it is an essential part of your anxious child's treatment, so it must be taken seriously; as a part of due diligence.

- **Read books about child anxiety and arm yourself with knowledge**

You must enlighten yourself about your child's disorder and keep your knowledge up to date. As your anxious child begins to receive medical and psychological treatment for their disorder, you may encounter many terms that you will need to lookup. Terms like dopamine, norepinephrine, and other neurotransmitters will be present or involved in some of the medication that your child's psychologist may prescribe for your anxious child. Ask your psychologist or therapist to explain them to you, and look them up yourself (At this stage, you may also need to disclose your child's known allergies. Do not hesitate to do so). Also, you should ask your child's psychologist or therapist to walk you through the step-by-step elements of their treatment plan for your child, as you want to be involved. As a matter of fact, you must be involved.

Now, we shall examine other frequently asked questions or FAQs about child anxiety:

- **How can you help your anxious child during a panic attack episode?**

Speak calmly to them. Say words like "breathe," "you're okay," "everything will be okay," or, if you're up for taking up some added responsibility and trust; "I've got you," "Mommy is here/Daddy is here…I won't let anything hurt you," "The spider won't get you, I've handled it, see?" (In which case, you actually have to handle it). Remind them to breathe. This part is very important as they may lose consciousness if the panic attack goes on for too long or is too severe. Make breathing easier for them by opening the windows and undoing the top few buttons of tight shirts. Make them put their heads between their knees to ease dizziness and get them some chocolate or juice. Singing or humming soothingly to them may also work. If you can't help them to get their panic attack under control after 5 – 10 minutes of doing all of this, call their psychologist or therapist at once or call an ambulance for them. Panic attacks are serious stuff, and aside from being clear indicators of an anxiety disorder, they may also be symptoms of other medical conditions.

- **Why does my child have anxiety?**

The precise answer to this question is unclear, but in earlier chapters – Chapter 3 to be exact – we have examined factors that may be responsible for anxiety in anxious children; factors like the biological factor, genetics and family factor and the environmental factor (You may want to revisit this chapter). Also, we made it quite clear that two or more of these factors may be in play in the life of any unique anxious child.

- **Does psychotherapy really work?**

Psychotherapy is the major method – or one of the major methods – that your child's psychologist may employ in the treatment of your child. As the name implies, it involves a lot of therapy. These sessions work mainly to uncover whatever underlying causes may be responsible for your child's anxiety, as well as how these discoveries may be utilized in their treatment plan. Psychotherapy has a considerably high success rate in treating mild to severe cases of anxiety, and the length or number of therapy sessions will depend on the estimated severity of each unique anxious child's condition. In some extreme cases, however, psychotherapy may be employed alongside other treatment methods such as medication.

- **Can my child really overcome child anxiety?**

Of course. Your anxious child absolutely can overcome their anxiety. They (children) are the ones that have the best chances of overcoming this disorder. As a matter of fact, if anyone can beat anxiety, your child can.

It may not be easy. Yet it is entirely possible (with the adequate response and the right kind of approach to their treatment.)

Chapter 8:
How You Should React In the Face of Progress (Or Setbacks)

Anxiety disorders are mental and psychological in nature, and so being, there will be good days and bad days when it comes to the effectiveness of any form of treatment. Positivity, of course, is an essential requirement on this journey. However, things may not pan out well quite as quickly as you think. I'm trying to say that as a parent or caregiver to an anxious child, it would not be prudent of you to expect a hasty recovery. It would be particularly unwise to set any kind of deadline for the complete eradication of your child's anxiety.

Why? Well, because these things take time.

A lot of parents and caregivers expect magic to happen as soon as their anxious child begins psychotherapy or medication, or any other form of treatment (or treatment plan which has been recommended by the medical professional). These parents do not remember to consider that extreme terror and irrational fear do not magically disappear just because you have started addressing or treating them. It is not that easy. It is a process that may be very difficult and long, depending on the severity of the anxiety of your unique anxious child. You should not dive into treatment for anxiety with your child expecting things to be easy. As a matter of fact, you should be wary if it appears to be; because, in this case, there may be an even higher chance of relapse as time and treatment progress.

The very nature of anxiety itself makes any form of treatment a work in progress, a process, something that will take some time. And no, I am not hinting at the duration of a few hours or days or even weeks (although the child's condition may likely improve within a short duration, following the commencement of treatment). I'm talking about a few months, at the very least.

The treatment of anxiety is something we have previously briefly examined. However, much as we have tried to paint clear pictures of children dealing with anxiety to parents and caregivers – and I would like to think that by now, we must have managed a reasonable degree of success at this – it would appear that we haven't given as much explanation regarding what the process of treating anxiety really looks like. Well, pay attention now, dear parent.

Anxiety disorders can be insidious in the sense that they work with fear and stress and that ever-present question, "What if?" Couple this with a child's boundless imagination, and you will have a very anxious one on your hands. The reasons for this disorder may not be well known, but oftentimes there is a cause or at least a trigger. For some children, this trigger is merely the fear of making a fool of themselves in front of their peers and other people. Still, when this fear is worked upon by anxiety, it may become social anxiety disorder or social phobia. For some, they might have lost a pet, or a favorite toy, or someone close to them, a grandparent or some relative perhaps.

The treatment of any form of anxiety disorder can be rough and taxing on both the anxious child and the parent or caregiver, and as implied earlier, there will be ups and downs. For this reason, it is important for parents and caregivers of anxious children to know how to behave in the face of progress (be it positive or negative).

In the instance of the child with separation anxiety disorder, good progress – such as finally being able to spend time apart from their parent or caregiver without crying or throwing a tantrum – is indeed a cause for celebration. However, the parent probably should not go too overboard. Of course, you should reward the anxious child (or recovering anxious child, in this case) with gifts or whatever incentive had been promised. But the exuberant parent or caregiver should manage their expectations. I'm not saying you shouldn't rejoice. Instead, I'm simply encouraging you to live in the moment. So, your child's treatment plan is working; congratulations. But along with that feeling of triumph, there may also be some expectation that "Ha! This is the way things will be from now on." Locate that expectation and can it. Put it away, far away, from your mind. Not because of the child – not really – but because of you. If you cannot learn to "manage" your expectation – to master it, and control it and not allow it to ride you – you may become a slave to it. And subsequently, it will place you on an emotional see-saw. You'll go up every time your child is obviously doing better, and then, every time the case is the exact opposite, you're likely to go down. And you may lash out at your child in frustration and anger. You must know all of these feelings are inevitable in the course of parenting (even if that child does not have anxiety), and what I have asked you to do may be impossible. However, you can control how you handle them. The next time your child with separation anxiety behaves well as you say your goodbyes and goes on to behave well for their babysitters or whoever you have entrusted them with, in your absence, rejoice and enjoy the triumph. Tell their psychologist. If, after that, they cry and throw tantrums when you leave, you can feel low. Still inform their psychologist and discuss it with the child. But never ever think that it is their fault or yours or even the child psychologist, particularly if you happen to have done your research on their methods, you've sought second opinions. You are in full agreement with everything. Instead, live in the moment this time and ask your child questions like: "What is wrong, Georgie (replace Georgie with the anxious child's name)? But you did so well the last time." Hear what they have to say and listen so that you can make necessary adjustments if need be. It may be that they think this particular babysitter is mean, or maybe something happened to them at school that brought their anxiety to the forefront. Whatever the reason may be – even if it is not one that they themselves can determine, or there appears to be no reason – lashing out at them in anger will not solve anything. As a matter of fact, such a reaction may even add to your child's anxiety.

Similarly, when a child with specific phobia doesn't exhibit extreme reactions to the object of their phobia, you should reward them; although, you may have to find some subtle way of doing this as calling the child's attention to this fact may – in certain cases – remind them of their fear or extreme anxiety towards that object. Instead, discuss the incident with their psychologist and listen to their recommendations for how you should move on. In the face of a relapse, however, you should also discuss it with their psychologist. If you wish to discuss it with your child, you must be calm and do so gently.

Conversely, in the instance of the anxious child receiving treatment for selective mutism, you must encourage any effort on their part to open the lines of communication with people outside their comfort zone. The decision has to be the child's own, so do not force them to speak to people when they are not ready. Do not talk down to them or speak about them as if they are not there – this is a common habit of parents of children with selective mutism – instead, encourage them gently and if they still do not (choose to) communicate, respect their choices. However, whenever they do go along with your gentle nudging or on the off chance that they take the initiative to speak to someone new – someone safe – take the triumph and live in the moment. If they make no further attempts to communicate with that individual after such an encounter, you may let them be. You may – should – also ask them about it using questions like: "You got on so well with Shirley the last time, Georgie (replace Georgie with the name of the anxious child). I noticed that you didn't say 'Hi' to her today. Is anything the matter?" Listen to them and try to talk it out as gently and as carefully as you can. However, in any case, you should always inform their psychologist about such instances and listen to their take. Instances like this may also hold true for anxious children with social phobia. In cases like this, when they manage to do well in a class presentation or make a friend and get invited to sleepovers and parties, rejoice with them and live in the moment. And if the exact opposite happens, then try to lighten the mood and cheer up your child. Better yet, give them what they need, be it space, time, or your easy and understanding silence. Be their friend and be their safe haven. You will surely be rewarded. And also importantly, always remember to inform their therapist or psychologist about these things.

Conversely, in cases where the anxious child suffers from panic disorders, congratulate and celebrate with them adequately and as proportionately as possible whenever they come into contact with triggers or triggering situations without experiencing a panic attack; particularly when they were able to hold off the symptoms by employing meditation, breathing exercises or other strategies that their therapist or psychologist may have recommended and taught to them. Do not lash out at them or scold them whenever it appears that they've relapsed or their condition is getting worse. Instead, speak gently to them and try not to burden them constantly with the weight of your own worries, as this may only add to their anxiety. Instead, try your possible best for your child.

Finally, in the case of a child with generalized anxiety disorder (GAD), proper parents or caregivers should endeavor to allow the child to grow and flourish by providing them with as much stability as possible. Children with generalized anxiety disorder will worry over anything and everything if their disorder is not well- managed, and this will probably make them very tired and physically fatigued easily. Parents of children like this must take care not to lash out at their anxious young ones as this may only stress them out and add to their anxiety. It may be difficult to keep calm in the face of the effects of this disorder and its possible effects on your child's life and school work. However, remember that you are not doing "nothing." You are not merely standing by and watching them suffer. No, you are talking to them about their fears in a gentle manner, you are giving them a shoulder to cry on and ears that care and listen, you are giving them a heart and mind that has their very best interests at heart, as well as the services of certified medical professionals. You are helping them, and as long as you are doing this and doing it well, to the utmost best of your ability and then some – without any coddling or drill sergeant-ing – well...then, you may live in the moment and encourage your anxious child to do the same; celebrating the highs and the lows (or, at least, enduring the lows with positivity and patience).

Ultimately no one can control how you react in the face of your child's progress in the face of anxiety and its treatment...no one except for you. You must react well, despite how you may be feeling. I'm not saying you should lie to them or pretend about your feelings, just acknowledge the situation, whatever it may be, face it head-on or with subtlety, and move on from it. Your child deserves that much. They are worthy of that much. And really, so are you, dear parent. Compassion is nearly always a two-way street. And you should endeavor to be compassionate to your anxious child in the face of the triumphant feeling of the highs or the frustration of the lows. So do try your best to temper your reactions with as much compassion, positivity, and patience as your anxious child truly needs at that moment, and be gracious. And if you falter and lose your cool. Well, don't make a habit of it. Be better, react better, next time— for your anxious child and for yourself.

Chapter 9:
The Importance of Patience and Positivity

Positivity is a precious state of mind that has been mentioned several times in this text; the reason being that it is an essential part of creating a suitable emotional and mental climate for a child who is dealing with anxiety.

You see, dear parent, if psychotherapy and other forms of treatment for anxiety are processes or marathon races, then positivity is the drive that keeps the runners – the anxious child, you (the parent or caregiver), and the medical professional(s); in this case – moving towards the finish line. More aptly put, positivity is not just the drive; it is the endurance, the stamina that keeps you fully committed to the race as you head to that finish line; even as your muscles hurt and every breath you take becomes shallower and more precious. Positivity makes the journey easy, even when it isn't. It makes things better somehow, no matter how difficult the process of overcoming child anxiety may be.

But the process of treating child anxiety is not a race, and there are so many reasons for this. For one, each unique anxious child is different, and so are their experiences and anxiety disorders. No two anxious children have exactly the same circumstances, experiences, triggers, and level of sensitivity to the same anxiety disorder. This is rather improbable – not impossible, but definitely rare – and since no two unique children are ever exactly the same anyway, in terms of behavior and personality (even if they are identical twins), it is rather unlikely for any two anxious children to overcome the same anxiety disorder in the same way. And so, parents and caregivers of anxious children have to constantly remind themselves to actually look at their own child during the treatment process. They have to see their own unique anxious child and see to their needs, instead of all the "success stories" that they might have read on the internet or heard through the grapevine. This requires patience.

And so, in the case of an anxious child with separation anxiety disorder, their parents or caregivers must exercise patience whenever their anxious children are throwing tantrums or acting out because it is time for them to say goodbye for a little while. I am not saying that you should not be firm with them, even as you explain to them why you must go. Only that you should do so in a gentle manner so as not to increase your anxious child's anxiety. Try to remember everything that we have discussed concerning how the child with separation anxiety feels at every point of departure and be patient with them. Do not lash out at them in anger or raise your voice or use scathing words. You must also remain positive. Your positivity serves an important role, as a reminder, because the optimism and – dare I say – expectation that things are going to get better as your child continues their treatment will help to keep you grounded, particularly during trying moments when your patience is being tested.

Similarly, in the instance of an anxious child with specific phobia, their parents and caregivers have to take special care to accommodate their needs, as there may be times when this may not be convenient. For instance, if your child is afraid of the dark, you may have to deal with higher electricity bills than normal during the duration of their anxiety disorder (which could last for a while). If they are afraid of thunderstorms, you may have to deal with sleepless nights on nights like that or calls from their school whenever it starts raining. If your anxious child is afraid of spiders, you may have to spend a lot more on housekeeping than you normally would and pay much closer attention to the cleanliness of your house, including books, crannies, and all the dark places. You may also need to start spending money on insect and spider repellants. And then, you may even have to prepare yourself to handle those arachnids yourself whenever your anxious child is about to have a panic attack episode, and you're the only one around. Quite simply put, as a parent or caregiver of a child with specific phobia anxiety disorder, you have to be willing to deal with the object of their extreme fear as well. And sometimes it may be inconvenient for you. However, you must exercise patience during these moments, as well as positivity. You must see such activities as part of the process of treating or at least managing your anxious child's anxiety, and you shouldn't lash out at them because of it.

Conversely, in the instance of a child with selective mutism, you must be patient with them whenever their anxiety disorder steals away their words. Do not try to force them to speak in moments like this, and do not put them on the spot either, as instances such as these could add to the child's anxiety and trigger panic attacks. One thing you can do to help your anxious child out during moments such as this – a strategy, so to speak – whenever you notice that they are being put or stuck in uncomfortable situations that may bring on their panic attacks is to try and lighten up the mood. In order to do this, you could start telling a story or divert people's attention away from your anxious child through some other means; this may help to deescalate the situation as well as slow down the build-up of panic in the mind of your child, at that moment. And the more subtle you are, the better. Aside from this, you may also give instructions to their teachers and other caregivers about not forcing your anxious child to talk by shouting at them, punishment, or through other scare tactics. This requires a lot of patience and positivity on the part of the parents or caregivers of the anxious child with selective mutism, as part of their job – the essence of trying to make things easier for the anxious child using this method – is to provide safe emotional and mental environments for them; to remove any sort of harsh or overtly undue pressure to speak, so that the anxious child may become less fearful and less anxious at the thought of doing it (speaking to people) outside their comfort zone.

Likewise, in the case of the child with social anxiety disorder or social phobia, they should not be forced to interact with others outside their comfort zone. Instead, they should be encouraged gently by their parents or caregivers and their therapist or psychologist to step out of their comfort zones, interact with others amongst their peers, and form friendships and other such desired bonds. This is because when such an anxious child is coerced or forced into interacting with others...well, such arrangements tend to backfire, and in the aftermath, your child may be left even more wary of social interaction and with a lot more anxiety. In fact, it is possible for such arrangements or situations to undo weeks, months, or even years of progress that the anxious child has made over the course of their treatment (e.g., psychotherapy and other forms). And so, for this reason, you must always remember to exercise patience, dear parent. Trust the process – the treatment process – or at least try to be positive about it.

Much of the same thing applies in the case of an anxious child with panic disorder. Patience is an attribute that parents and caregivers of such children must learn and display in abundance because of the nature of this child's anxiety disorder. In the course of treating panic disorder, there may be a few ups and downs; moments when the treatment appears to be working flawlessly, and then some episodes of panic attacks that may or may not be worse than before. An anxiety disorder like this is not likely to disappear overnight (although this does happen), particularly if your young child is above the range of ages 5 – 7. In many cases, the road to recovery is a long and tedious one, and very rarely does it lie straight. And so, parents and caregivers of anxious children such as this must learn to exercise patience as well as positivity. You must remain calm in the face of their own chaotic emotions, and you must always be on the lookout for them with a clear head. When they suffer from panic attacks – a major symptom of this particular disorder – you must learn to put your own fears in perspective and keep yourself from being overwhelmed by them until your child is fine. Your first priority in these precious moments is to first help your child, make sure that they are breathing, that they are conscious and that their heart rate is back to normal. And then, you have to get them checked out at the hospital or by a professional and inform their therapist. And when such a situation is something that you potentially have to deal with regularly (even as your anxious child undergoes treatment) or you have an anxious child with clearly defined triggers who just wouldn't stay away from those triggers...well, then, dear parent, you will need to be patient indeed. However, positivity can be a shield.

The instance of an anxious child with generalized anxiety disorder (GAD) is not so different from all that has been said this far in this chapter. Their parents or caregivers also need to exercise a lot of patience where they (the anxious child) are concerned. In this case, however, the parents' patience and positivity are required mostly for the purpose of sparing the child's feelings. As we have examined in earlier chapters, the anxious child with GAD experiences anxiety about everything, at least about a wide range of things of different varieties. And so, your patience and positivity will go a long way in unburdening their minds and keeping them free of any added stress or anxiety.

Positivity and patience, these two virtues must go hand in hand in the character of a proper parent or caregiver of the anxious child. As a proper parent or caregiver to an anxious child, you should always remain hopeful about the future progress of your child – and be positive – even as you endure the present (with patience). You must combine these two attributes, and you must do this for your anxious child because it will be expected of you as a parent or caregiver of a child (with or without an anxiety disorder).

When children are in pain, they usually ask for their parents because the dynamics of parenthood and childhood are linked in such a way that children will always look to their parents for the answers. This is often true even for older children and for many adult children. No matter how old we are or how old we grow up to be, many of us still hold our parents in certain regard; it is almost reverent and godlike. It may not even matter how we see them as individuals; we just believe – or used to believe – that as long as they are with us and by our sides, everything will be okay. And so, this is the responsibility that has now fallen unto you as a parent or caregiver to a child (especially one with an anxiety disorder). You must be patient – with them and with yourself – and you must be calm. You must encourage them, and you must also encourage yourself. Quite simply put, you must be their safe place, or at least, you must provide a mental and emotional climate that is safe enough for nurturing your unique anxious child. It won't be easy for you as an individual, but at the end of the day, you will come to know them better, help them become better, and you both will be better for it.

One thing you need to know about child anxiety is that it is not fun, especially for the anxious child, and with all that chaos that is going on inside them – cutesy of their anxiety disorder – they are suffering. I know that this isn't a pretty picture to paint for any parent or caregiver – the fact that their child is suffering – but that is what it is, a fact. Now, the severity of it or how true it is in terms of levels and degrees will likely vary from child to child. However, no matter what level your child finds themselves on the anxiety severity spectrum, it still isn't ideal. And wherever chaos exists, there is always going to be a need for peace. Your child may not realize it, they may not even feel it but, eventually, they may come to feel the full brunt of this need; particularly during episodes of panic attacks or whenever they feel such episodes coming on. Consequently, the child may begin to act out or engage in certain activities or behaviors in a rather misguided effort to seek out peace. Some, especially those with social anxiety disorder and selective mutism, may cut classes or avoid school. Others may choose to self-medicate or self-harm. They may choose unhealthy outlets for their anxiety, and ultimately this may hinder their development and the progress of their treatment. One way to prevent this is to step up for them as a parent or caregiver. Emotionally, mentally and in every good way that you – and they – can think of. Give them positivity and patience; give them peace in their own homes and a safe haven to lay their head upon, and time will surely reward you.

Chapter 10:
What You Must Do When Your Child Finally Stops Being Anxious

When your child finally stops being anxious, you might not realize it immediately. The signs of recovery from disorders like anxiety may be subtle at times, particularly in young children, especially when the emotional and mental groundwork is being laid. You see, it isn't always as it is in the movies, when there's a defining moment of clarity, when someone says a single word or has a life-changing conversation with the young child with anxiety, and suddenly, they get cured. No, most of the time, complete healing occurs over time, as constant and repetitive efforts of psychotherapy, and/or other treatments (such as medication), and adequate care get laid upon each other over and over again, unto the raw form that is the anxious child, like raw cement. Cement takes time to form, to set, and so does healing in an anxious child.

Setbacks will come and go because notwithstanding the level of severity of your young child's anxiety, they (young children) still have some of the very best chances of making a full recovery from anxiety disorders.
And so, at the end of the day, when treatment and everything else pays off, what else is there to do?
Well, there are many, many things that parents and caregivers of anxious children – or rather, previously anxious children – still have to watch out for as their young child continues to grow and develop.

First and foremost, avoid unnecessary reminders of that period of your child's life as much as possible. This step doesn't usually call for extreme actions like getting rid of pictures, toys, and photo albums. No,– at least, not unless this is what your certified child psychologist has recommended, and you happen to be in full agreement with it after you might have sought a second opinion on the issue – because you don't want to go leaving a hole. The goal here, the goal of not reminding your child of this trying period for some time, is not to create a hole or chasm in their hearts and minds; naturally, many humans forget things, children especially. As a matter of fact, many of us – adults – cannot remember a lot of things about our early childhood, especially when they have to do with pure, concrete facts about our daily lives at that period in time. Instead, we tend to remember feelings, fleeting pieces and warm bits of memories, swirls of colors, and faces of childhood friends that blur together in our minds like wet paintings made of watercolor. We forget, and so, your young child may also forget this period of their lives. Or, over time, the memories may lose their intensity, and they will fade. Later on in life, by the time they become your age, they may have even forgotten the faces of their child psychologist. And this is something that will probably happen naturally with time.

However, if you constantly keep reminding your child of this period – or of their anxieties – as parents are prone to do out of concern or whenever they want to make a point (or sometimes due to carelessness or as a result of poor humor), then the child may have a reason to keep holding on to those memories long after they ought to have faded.

Aside from this, you must continue to watch your child. Do not immediately bring it to their attention when you first begin to notice a significant lessening of their symptoms or anxiety. First, take the time to watch and observe. Study their new behavior and ask yourself questions as you compare it to how they were before.

In the case of the anxious child with separation anxiety disorder, try not to call too much attention to remarkable changes in their behavior – or, more aptly put, their condition – except for the purpose of praising their good and improved condition and to reward them. As a parent or caregiver to a child such as this, do not make snide remarks about their progress or belittle it in anyway. Your anxious child has finally overcome their disorder and harsh reminders such as comments or remarks like: "It's about time you stopped being such a baby, Georgie" (you may replace it with the name of the unique anxious child if you so wish), may only remind the child of the reason for their SAD (separation anxiety disorder) in the first place. Subsequently, if lingering fears or feelings of their form of child anxiety disorder persist, they may likely be hesitant to bring them to your notice. And the stress of having to hide these feelings may result in a lot of stress that may only worsen over time, potentially leading to a relapse in their condition or – in many cases – the development of another form of anxiety disorder. This scenario is something that ought to be avoided and prevented at all costs, so try, dear parent. Try to be happy for your anxious child and their progress; allow them to thrive in it, and it will likely last.

In the instance of the anxious child with specific phobia, the fact that you – their parent or caregiver – have now noticed that they no longer the object of their anxiety does not mean that you may now begin experimenting by intentionally over-exposing them to those things. For example, it would be juvenile of you, as a proper parent or caregiver, to test out your theories by putting a spider on your anxious child's bed, just to check if indeed they have gotten over their specific phobia of spiders. Or to simulate the sound of a thunderstorm – with an app or something when it is raining – if your anxious child is (or was) extremely anxious about lightning and thunder. In the same vein, you should not start turning off the light wherever they go, simply because they seem to have gotten over their fear of the dark. It is very important for you not to…well, push your luck as much as you can, dear parent, in the face of your anxious child's – or rather former anxious child's – considerable and remarkable progress at overcoming their specific anxiety. As much as you can, try to accept their progress, celebrate it, and live in the moment. And do not do any of what we have classified as "pushing your luck" in the face of your child's progress; to avoid a relapse.

In the instance of a child who has overcome their selective mutism, the parents or caregivers of such an anxious child should do everything within their power to still respect the child's verbally reserved nature – or former verbally reserved nature – by not pushing them into conversation with everybody they see; like every peer and every neighbor they happen to stumble upon or interact with. What this simply means is that while the anxious child's remarkable progress is a great thing and something to be celebrated, as their parent or caregiver, you should try to keep in mind that talking is a verbal exercise, and it can be taxing. In this case, in the face of this progress, it is not your job to let your child exhaust themselves or strain themselves mentally under the guise of showing how well they are doing. In some cases – many cases, actually – it is the anxious child themselves that does this over-exertion in terms of verbal communication. And in such instances, it can come as quite a shock to parents and caregivers to find their formerly anxious child with selective mutism becoming a chatterbox after they finally overcome their anxiety disorder. But even in this scenario, parents and caregivers must watch over their child and try as much as possible to make them feel comfortable outside their comfort zone so that there will be no occurrence of a relapse.

Similarly, after the recovery of an anxious child with social anxiety disorder or social phobia, the parents and caregivers of such children must still exercise caution. Of course, there is every chance – every possibility of the anxious child (or formerly anxious child) – going on to live the rest of their lives without the shadow of their child anxiety looming over them, and many of them may later grow up to be some of the most charismatic and confident people (or even teenagers) that you will ever meet, parents must keep in might that their might have been an underlying cause for their child's anxiety and that that reason must still be addressed, even if the anxious child appears to have gotten over it. Until that underlying reason is sufficiently addressed, all the (previously) anxious child's confidence may still be under threat. And in certain cases, the reoccurrence of their anxiety might happen, and their condition may even present itself as another form of the condition, such as panic disorder or selective mutism.

Conversely, when a child has recovered from their panic disorder (finally), you must try as much as possible to still avoid their triggers. In previous chapters – and even earlier on in this particular chapter – we stated that you should not "push your luck" by constantly exposing your (previously) anxious child continuously to their anxiety triggers. This same thing applies in this case. As much as possible, still continue to observe your (formerly) anxious child because the strength or effectiveness of their recovery may rely solely on how well they handle themselves in the face of their likely triggers for episodes of panic attacks or in situations that make them uncomfortable.

Finally, when it comes to the recovery of an anxious child with GAD...well, there is no easy advice or recommendation because worries are perhaps an inescapable part of life. As humans, as a species, we are constantly chasing after something, be it our goals, dreams, or even peace of mind. We are constantly holding on to things like our values, beliefs, and philosophies. "What if we make mistakes and we are not able to make our goals or dreams come true?" "What if somewhere along the way, we lose sight of our values and forget who we are?" These are some of the big questions that have the power to guide our every step. And then, there are the small – or seemingly small – decisions that we make every day and the many ways that they too can influence us or change the course of our lives. And then, of course, there are the things that we can't control, like other people's behavior, the weather, our bosses' moods...so many tiny little things that we can choose to worry about (and sometimes, it seems like it's not even our choice to make. We just worry). And so, for these reasons and many more, the parents of children who have overcome GAD must help their children see the good sides of every bad situation, the stability that exists in every chaotic scenario, and of course, the precious things that will never change; like your unconditional love for them or other own uniqueness. Quite simply put, you must help your (formerly) anxious child recover by teaching them to live. To enjoy the moments and do the best that they can.

That is positivity.

Conclusion

"(A) Calm mind brings inner strength and self-confidence, so that's very important for good health." – Dalai Lama

Finally, we have come to the end of this book, and it has been a journey indeed. The above quote by the Dalai Lama simply encompasses the purpose of this book and the information in it. A calm mind is a mind that is free of anxiety, and it is essential for your child's good health (as well as yours), and this is the truth.

At this stage, I would like to remind you of the content in the section titled "How to Get the Most Out of This Book." You must read, meditate and apply as much as you can, and hopefully, this book will be of great help to you as you parent your unique child with anxiety.

Chin up, dear parent, and remember, there is still much progress ahead.

www.ingramcontent.com/pod-product-compliance
Lightning Source LLC
Chambersburg PA
CBHW071528080526
44588CB00011B/1596